CRIME AND DETECTION

HATE CRIMES

Crime and Detection series

CRIME AND DETECTION

HATE CRIMES

JOHN WRIGHT

MASON CREST PUBLISHERS
www.masoncrest.com

Mason Crest Publishers Inc.
370 Reed Road
Broomall, PA 19008
(866) MCP-BOOK (toll free)
www.masoncrest.com

First printing

1 2 3 4 5 6 7 8 9 10

Library of Congress Cataloging-in-Publication Data on file at the Library of Congress

ISBN 1-59084-379-7

Editorial and design by
Amber Books Ltd.
Bradley's Close
74–77 White Lion Street
London N1 9PF
www.amberbooks.co.uk

Project Editor: Michael Spilling
Design: Floyd Sayers
Picture Research: Natasha Jones

Printed and bound in Malaysia

CONTENTS

Introduction

From the moment in the Book of Genesis when Cain's envy of his brother Abel erupted into violence, crime has been an inescapable feature of human life. Every society ever known has had its own sense of how things ought to be, its deeply held views on how men and women should behave. Yet in every age there have been individuals ready to break these rules for their own advantage: they must be resisted if the community is to thrive.

This exciting and vividly illustrated new series sets out the history of crime and detection from the earliest times to the present day, from the empires of the ancient world to the towns and cities of the 21st century. From the commandments of the great religions to the theories of modern psychologists, it considers changing attitudes toward offenders and their actions. Contemporary crime is examined in its many different forms: everything from racial hatred to industrial espionage, from serial murder to drug trafficking, from international terrorism to domestic violence.

The series looks, too, at the work of those men and women entrusted with the task of overseeing and maintaining the law, from judges and court officials to police officers and other law enforcement agents. The tools and techniques at their disposal are described and vividly illustrated, and the ethical issues they face concisely and clearly explained.

All in all, the *Crime and Detection* series provides a comprehensive and accessible account of crime and detection, in theory and in practice, past and present.

CHARLIE FULLER

Executive Director, International Association of Undercover Officers

Left: *The Eternal Jew* is the most famous Nazi propaganda film. This 1937 poster for the movie portrays Jews as money lenders, Bolsheviks, and slave drivers. The movie depicts the Jews as a corrupt people who have taken over the world through their control of banking and commerce.

People Who Hate

Most crimes involve some type of hate. A "hate crime," however, has become a specialized term for a criminal act committed against someone from a minority or "different" group. Crimes like this have always been committed and even influenced the course of history. Three examples are the Romans persecuting Christians, the white settlers taking land from Native Americans, and the Nazis murdering some six million Jews during World War II.

The world is still saddened and changed by hate crimes, as Americans experienced on September 11, 2001, one of the darkest days in our history. Those who commit hate crimes are often racists, or they might fear and hate such people as foreigners or homosexuals. Minorities can also commit crimes based on their own prejudices. Victims of hate crimes can be individuals, groups, companies, or other organizations. Various hate crime laws may be worded differently, but most are like the 1969 federal law that protects Americans from crimes committed because of "race, color, religion, or national origin." According to state laws, hate crimes can be done for other reasons, too, such as cultural or ethnic background, **gender**, sexual orientation, politics, social class, age, and physical or mental disability.

HOW TO RECOGNIZE A HATE CRIME

Many of these crimes involve **harassment** and **intimidation**, like calling people an abusive racial name or sending hate mail to them. Another form is property damage, from spraying graffiti on a house to burning down a

Left: More than 1,000 Jewish demonstrators gather in Anderlecht, Belgium, three weeks after a synagogue was firebombed there on April 1, 2002. Their sign compares the recent anti-Semitism with Nazi atrocities in 1938.

The expansion of the United States led to many crimes against Native Americans. This painting depicts U.S. cavalry using force against the Modoc people, who refused to give up their land on the West Coast.

church. The most extreme crime is personal assault, which may become murder. Hate crimes are particularly unpleasant because they terrorize an entire targeted community. Hate speech might also do this, but it is protected under the Constitution's First Amendment. This has probably helped increase the many hate sites on the Internet.

Hate crimes happen because of a number of reasons. They are based on prejudice, racial **stereotypes**, and ignorance, and rumors can strengthen these wrong opinions. Hate crimes are more likely when the races live in **segregated** areas or attend segregated schools. Particular reasons for hate crimes might be the economic betterment of a minority group or competition for jobs, housing, or education. They often occur because the attackers are under the influence of alcohol or drugs. **Zero tolerance** is the best method of dealing with such attacks, handling even the smallest incidents as crimes. If they are not dealt with quickly, they can become more severe or increase in number.

Hate crimes are difficult to solve because the criminal is usually a

The Nazis rounded up and murdered Jewish families throughout Europe, especially in Poland and in Russia. In one of the greatest crimes in history, about six million Jews were put to death before the Allies defeated Germany in 1945.

Hate crimes have grown through the years in cities around the world. This confrontation with police in London in 1993 involved Asian youths protesting a rally by the right-wing, anti-immigrant British National Party.

stranger to the victim, and the attack is done randomly or impulsively. Sometimes, an attack is done in error, as in a person's wrong belief that the victim is Jewish, but this is still recorded as a hate crime. Another major problem is that this type of crime often goes unreported. In 2002, Northeastern University in Boston released its survey of Massachusetts high schools, which revealed only 3.5 percent of the victims of hate crimes reported them to the police, and more than 30 percent told no one.

A particularly vicious type of hate crime is one committed by a law enforcement officer or some other official, such as a mayor, council member, or judge. These unlawful acts are said to be committed "under color of law." This legal term means the crimes are done using the official's apparent right under the law. Federal punishment for this is severe and can include life imprisonment or execution if the victim was killed.

OFFERING PROTECTION

The first modern federal law that offered protection from hate crimes involved **racism**. The FBI used the Civil Rights Act of 1964 that year to investigate the murders of three black civil rights workers in Mississippi, which led to seven white men being sent to prison. In 1968, Congress passed a new law that was more specific, naming crimes directed at individuals because of their race, color, religion, or national origin. Then, in 1990, the Hate Crimes Statistics Act was passed, directing the FBI to collect and count such crimes. (This act was the first federal one to use the term "hate crimes.")

A Hate Crimes Sentencing Enhancement Act was enacted in 1994 to increase the penalties for crimes against individuals because of their "actual or perceived race, color, religion, national origin, ethnicity, gender, disability, or sexual orientation." These laws are also known as bias (prejudice) laws.

In 1998, a Hate Crimes Prevention Act was introduced in Congress and was still under debate in 2002. If it becomes law, the federal government will, for the first time, be allowed to assist local investigations and prosecutions of crimes involving the victim's sexual orientation, gender, or disability. The law will also do away with restrictions that now permit federal help only if the crime occurs when the victim is doing an activity protected by the U.S. government, such as voting or attending a public school. It has great support, but several groups are opposing it. The executive director of the Traditional Values Coalition has said, "We shouldn't label some crimes more hateful than other crimes to advance a political agenda."

Under federal law, the FBI can investigate crimes based on prejudice against race, religion, disability, or ethnic and national origin. (Sexual orientation has not yet been added, so those crimes must be handled at the local level by the city, state, or county police.) The FBI has three programs concerning hate crimes: the Civil Rights Program focuses on individuals or small groups committing hate crimes; the Domestic Terrorism Program investigates crimes committed by organized groups for political or social reasons; and the Criminal Justice Information Services collects hate crime data nationwide.

ENFORCING THE LAW

The U.S. Department of Justice has a Civil Rights Division that also enforces federal civil rights laws involving hate crimes. Its Criminal Section prosecutes cases of violence against citizens and noncitizens alike. The U.S. Attorney General's Office has a Hate Crimes Working Group, which has developed a model for state and local groups to use in combating all types of hate crimes.

The FBI is one federal agency taking part in Hate Crimes Working Groups around the country. These are composed of representatives from different communities, including ethnic groups, law enforcement officers, and teachers. A good regional example is the Northern Ohio Hate Crimes Working Group.

Poverty and inequality have caused race riots in America's large urban areas. These include the Watts section of Los Angeles in 1965 and Washington, D.C., and other cities after Martin Luther King, Jr.'s assassination in 1968.

HATE CRIME STATISTICS

When the Hate Crime Statistics Act became law in 1990, the FBI began recording the numbers and types of hate crimes occurring in each state. In 2000, 11,690 law enforcement agencies in 48 states and the District of Columbia provided this information voluntarily to the FBI's Uniform Crime Reporting (UCR) Program. Although many crimes go unreported, the annual totals highlight the national problem and give a good indication of crime trends.

During 2000, the FBI recorded 8,063 hate crimes involving 9,924 victims and 7,530 known offenders (4,847 were white and 1,411 black). Nineteen victims were murdered, 10 of these because of racial bias, six because of ethnic or national origin, two for sexual orientation, and one because of religious bias. The most common crime, however, was intimidation, accounting for 53.7 percent of crimes against people and 34.9 percent of all crimes. Businesses, religious groups, and other institutions were the targets of 1,685 of the offenses.

State, county, and local authorities prosecute most hate crimes. In 2002, 43 states had passed hate laws. New Jersey is considered a model state for reporting and responding to hate crimes. Its Office of Bias Crime and Community Relations helps law enforcement agencies investigate and prosecute crimes. The states without such laws are Arkansas, Hawaii, Indiana, Kansas, New Mexico, South Carolina, and Wyoming.

At the county level, a prime example is Los Angeles County in California, which has a Hate Crimes Suppression Unit and also a Commission on Human Relations that operates a Network Against Hate Crimes with community groups and individuals. In Maryland, the Montgomery County

Police were confronted with numerous protest riots in 1992, such as this one in Atlanta, Georgia, after a court found four Los Angeles policemen not guilty of brutality in the beating of the African American motorist Rodney King.

Human Relations Commission supports hate crime victims, offering translations into English if needed, and accompanying people to court. It also works to eliminate the prejudices of youths who commit hate crimes. One of the good local programs is the Chicago Police Department. Its many units work together to tackle hate crimes, including the Civil Rights Unit,

Hate lived on in a Nazi swastika near Zernikow, Germany. In the late 1930s, a local man planted the trees that revealed the sign when their leaves changed color in the fall. Discovered in 1992, the trees have since been felled.

Detective Division, and Neighborhood Relations Division.

The problem is also discussed at special conferences. The International Association of Chiefs of Police held a "Hate Crime in America Summit" at its headquarters in Alexandria, Virginia, in 1998. The Summit produced 46 recommendations on understanding and preventing hate crimes and how to respond to them. It also drew up a Law Enforcement Action Agenda to help police combat hate crimes. Another example is the Hate Crime Symposium held in 2002 at the University of Michigan.

COMBATING HATE CRIMES WORLDWIDE

Hate crimes are a worldwide problem. In 2001, the United Nations held a "World Conference Against Racism, Racial Discrimination, Xenophobia, and Associated Intolerance." That same year, the World Council of Churches began a project entitled "Churches in Europe: Initiatives to Overcome Racism, **Xenophobia**, and Racial Violence."

Examples of hate crimes can be found in every country. The German government acknowledged a 40 percent rise in these crimes in 2000, to 13,753. That same year, an Australian was convicted of murdering two homosexual men, a storekeeper and a former politician. In 2001, in Glasgow, Scotland, a Turkish refugee was stabbed and killed in a racial attack. The British government had housed 1,500 **asylum seekers** in Glasgow, and 70 were victims of racial attacks in a 14-month period.

After the terrorist attacks on the United States on September 11, 2001, Muslims in every part of Europe became targets of racist abuse and attacks. In 2002, neo-Nazis in Russia attacked several foreigners in Moscow. French **synagogues** suffered a wave of arson attacks in response to increased violence in the Israeli-Palestine conflict in Israel. Blacks in Zimbabwe and South Africa attacked white farmers, while Indonesia experienced attacks against its ethnic Chinese minority. And in Spain, in July 2002 alone, Basque separatists murdered two police officers and a local politician in the north of the country.

COMMENTS ON HATE AND CRIMES

Warnings about hate crimes and prejudice have come from many American leaders:

"I believe that tolerance and respect must be taught to all our children, because too many young minds and souls are lost to hate."
President George W. Bush

"All Americans deserve protection from hate. Nothing is more important to our country's future than our standing together against intolerance, prejudice, and violent **bigotry**."
Former President, Bill Clinton

"These crimes are different because they are based on prejudice and hatred, which gives rise to crimes that have not a single victim, but are intended to dehumanize a whole group of people."
Former Vice President, Al Gore

"Hate crimes are a form of terrorism. They have a psychological and emotional impact that extends far beyond the victim. They threaten the entire community, and undermine the ideals on which the nation was founded."
Senator Edward Kennedy

"Hate crimes are a plague to the very fabric of our nation, and none of us are safe until all of us are safe."
Jesse Jackson (pictured), civil rights leader

"If you're beaten up because you're black or gay or Jewish, it's more than a simple assault. Hate crimes are terrorism."
Senator Vincent Fort

Family and friends attend the funeral of Yaakov Aminov, 46, at Yad Avraham Synagogue in Los Angeles, July 7, 2002. Aminov was one of three persons killed when a Muslim fanatic fired at crowds near the Israeli El Al airline ticket counter on July 4 at Los Angeles International Airport.

الدعاء المستجاب
من القرآن الكريم
وصحيح السنة
فوج کو اپنے اڈے
مت دو -
ملیر ٹاؤن

Religious Hatred

We usually think of religious conflict as something that belongs to history. However, the terrorist attacks of September 11, 2001, show how people use the name of religion even today to justify their evil acts. Certainly, history is full of battles caused by the clash of different religions. Many are described in the Old Testament of the Bible. Christians were thrown to the lions in ancient Rome when its citizens continued to believe in many gods as opposed to one. The Crusades in the 12th and 13th centuries cost thousands of lives as Christians battled against Muslims for the Holy Land in Palestine. A Children's Crusade was even launched in 1212, but was a great failure, with many children dying en route and others sold into slavery.

Since Roman times, many nations have persecuted Jewish people, often saying this was because the Jews crucified Christ, although reasons that are more obvious were the Jews' different religious and cultural practices or their financial successes. This hatred of Jews is called anti-Semitism. By the ninth century, Jews were not allowed to own property in Europe, so many began loaning money, which Christians were banned from doing. During the Crusades, Christians murdered thousands of Jews and forced them into ghettos (restricted districts). The English expelled Jews in 1209, as did the French in 1306. The worst outrage was the Nazis' mass killings during the Holocaust. Even after the Jewish people formed their own nation of Israel, they have been under constant threat and attack by Arab neighbors who practice the religion of Islam.

Left: A child holds up a Koran as he joins a protest against the United States that was held on September 23, 2001, in Karachi, Pakistan. Prejudice most often begins at a very early age, with children unquestioningly taking on the beliefs of their parents.

COLONIAL RACE CRIMES

Although many colonists came to America for religious freedom, they were often prejudiced against other religions. The Puritans who settled in Massachusetts denied the vote to people who were not members of their church. They persecuted the Baptists and Quakers, passing laws against them and even executing some. Salem, Massachusetts, was also a center for a different type of religious crime, the execution of people who supposedly practiced witchcraft. In 1692, after several young girls claimed they had been bewitched, the community executed 14 women and 6 men, and several more "witches" died in prison. Early settlers also considered Native Americans to be heathens who needed to be converted from their own religions to Christianity. More brutality occurred in Central and South

Religious hate crimes go far back in history. All the great religions have had leaders who became victims of persecution. In this illustration, St. Istvan (Stephen), a Hungarian Franciscan, is tortured by Muslim Tartars.

American settlers had little tolerance for the "heathen" religions of Native American people. Much pressure was applied to convince Native Americans to renounce their traditional religions and be baptized as Christians.

America in the 16th century when the Spanish *conquistadores* (meaning conquerors) murdered Aztecs and Incas who would not become Christians.

An old and still familiar problem among Christians has been the prejudice between Roman Catholics and Protestants. In England, Henry VIII broke with the Roman Catholic Church in 1534, establishing his own church, and closing at least 800 monasteries. His eldest daughter, Mary I, then became queen. She was a Roman Catholic and persecuted Protestants, burning to death some 300 of them and earning the nickname of "Bloody Mary." When she died, her Protestant sister, Elizabeth I, took the throne and persecuted Roman Catholics, even having her Roman Catholic cousin, Mary, Queen of Scots, beheaded. Other Roman Catholic-Protestant conflicts raged throughout Europe, including the Thirty Years War, which began in 1618 because Ferdinand II of Austria wanted to force his Roman Catholic religion on others.

THE SAD CASE OF NORTHERN IRELAND

The Roman Catholic-Protestant argument provides us with a bridge to religious hate crimes today. The only true national violence between the

A rally in Northern Ireland takes place on the 25th anniversary of "Bloody Sunday," when British soldiers opened fire, killing 13 civil rights marchers on January 30, 1972. Visible are two of the large portraits of the victims.

THE IRISH REPUBLICAN ARMY

The Irish Republican Army (IRA) was first set up as a guerrilla organization in 1919 in Ireland to fight against British rule. When Ireland gained independence in 1922, part of its northern region chose to remain in the United Kingdom as Northern Ireland. The IRA, a Catholic organization, turned to terrorism in Northern Ireland to break with the United Kingdom and become part of the Republic of Ireland.

They bombed English cities and Protestant areas of Northern Ireland until peace talks in 1997, led by the former U.S. Senator George Mitchell (whose father was Irish). The IRA agreed to disarm, and Northern Ireland's own Protestant-Roman Catholic government came into being in 1999.

two religions in modern times has been in Northern Ireland. The two religions are highly politicized, because the Protestants want Northern Ireland to remain part of the United Kingdom, while the minority Roman Catholics would like to be united with Ireland. Roman Catholics were not allowed to hold public offices for many years and suffered other discriminations. They began a campaign of violence in the 1960s, led by the terrorist Irish Republican Army (IRA), which murdered Protestants and bombed buildings in Northern Ireland and England. In response, the Protestants created their own terrorist paramilitary groups. When the IRA announced an end to its violence in 1994, more than 3,000 Protestants and Roman Catholics had been killed.

In recent American history, hate crimes against Roman Catholics have been less violent, but certainly just as hurtful. Anti-Catholic feelings were strong in the United States in the 19th century, since some people thought the Pope could influence the political views of Roman Catholics. A political party called the American Party, or "Know-Nothing Party," made its members promise never to vote for a Roman Catholic. When Democratic candidate Al Smith became the first Roman Catholic to run for president in 1928 and was defeated by Republican Herbert Hoover, many Americans thought a Roman Catholic would never lead the nation. This was proved wrong when John F. Kennedy was elected in 1960, but even during that race, many people wondered if Kennedy's first loyalty would be to his church rather than his country. In one speech to Protestant clergy during the campaign, Kennedy said, "No Catholic prelate would tell the President, should he be a Catholic, how to act, and no Protestant minister should tell his parishioners for whom to vote."

ANTI-CATHOLICISM IN THE U.S. TODAY

Hate crimes against American Roman Catholics, who make up about one-quarter of the U.S. population, mostly involve intimidation and harassment. The racist Ku Klux Klan, known for burning the Christian

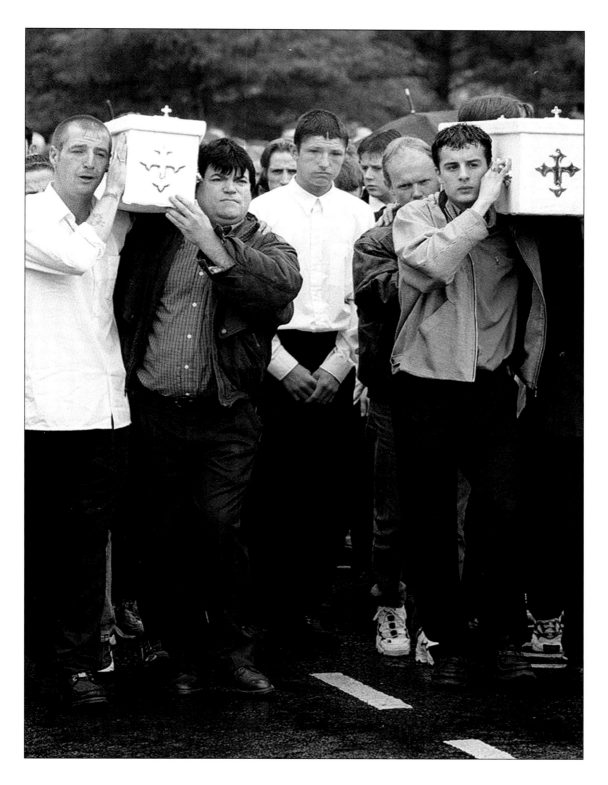

The coffins of three brothers murdered in an arson attack are carried down a street in Northern Ireland. John Dillion (far left), their father, assists at this sad occasion, one of the many funerals caused by religious hatred.

symbol of a cross and persecuting African Americans, has long put out **propaganda** against Roman Catholics and Jews. Internet sites by such individuals and organizations have increased, some promoting religious arguments trying to convert Roman Catholics, and others promoting pure hate messages about the dangers of Catholicism.

Anti-Catholic statements also come from unexpected sources. In 2000, a Baptist church in Vista, California, distributed outside high schools leaflets that called Roman Catholic Communion wafers "death cookies" because Roman Catholic rituals are not found in the Bible. During the Republican presidential primaries that year, members of his own party accused George W. Bush of being anti-Catholic for speaking in South Carolina at Bob Jones University, which had labeled Roman Catholicism a "cult." In 2001, a member of the Seventh-Day Adventists put up a highway billboard near Medford, Oregon, calling the Pope "the Antichrist."

Most religious groups, however, have helped lead campaigns against hate crimes. One example is the Executive Council of the Episcopal Church, which has taken a strong stand against hate crimes, urging Congress to include gender, sexual orientation, and disability in new laws. The Council passed a resolution calling on the "whole church to commit itself at every level to work for the eradication of hate crimes in America."

WORLDWIDE ANTI-SEMITISM

Violent hate crimes are committed worldwide against Jews, who, as mentioned earlier, have been targets of racists for centuries. Neo-Nazis and other racist groups have continually vandalized Jewish gravestones and painted Nazi swastika symbols on synagogues and other Jewish property.

Violence against Jewish targets greatly increased at the beginning of the 21st century as the Israeli-Palestinian conflict grew. The World Jewish Congress warned in 2002 that the number of anti-Semitic attacks in Europe was the highest since World War II. The attackers tended to be Palestinians, other Arabs, and their supporters. France has had a wave of hate-crime violence against Jews, who number 600,000, compared with five million Muslims in that nation. One French government report showed an increase in personal attacks on Jews, from one case in 1998 to 116 in 2000. These often occur in Paris suburbs where the two groups live together in poor housing projects. Attackers have broken the windows of Jewish residents and sprayed graffiti, such as "Dirty Jew," on their houses and cars. In April 2002, the European Union pledged to "step up preventative action and the fight against racist violence and anti-Semitism."

In 2002, many other countries had an upsurge in anti-Semitism. These

Burning crosses are symbols of the Ku Klux Klan. The secret organization was formed to terrorize African Americans. It has added Catholics, Jews, and others to its hate list, but the Klan's membership has fallen.

THE ISRAELI-ARAB CONFLICT

The United Nations took possession of part of Palestine in 1947 to create a homeland for the Jewish people who had suffered six million deaths at the hands of the Nazis. The rest of the Middle East belonged to Arab countries, so this brought the Jewish and Islamic religions face-to-face. The following year, Israel proclaimed its independence and the forces of Egypt, Jordan, Syria, Lebanon, Iraq, and Saudi Arabia promptly invaded. Israel defeated this attack and, in 1967, won the "Six-Day War."

A new wave of terrorism began in 2000, when Palestinian suicide bombers began attacking Israeli cities and Israel's army invaded and bombarded Palestinian areas, almost leveling the refugee camp at Jenin in 2002 (see picture). On April 2 that year, more than 200 Palestinians, including terrorists, fled into Bethlehem's Church of the Nativity, believed to be the site of Jesus' birth, and Israeli forces surrounded it. The siege lasted five weeks until an agreement was reached to deport 13 of the terrorists to other European nations and send 26 militants to the Palestinian district of Gaza.

A Jewish boy looks through a broken window at a synagogue in Kiev, Ukraine, on April 14, 2002. Dozens of local youths had stoned the building's windows the previous night in a vicious anti-Semitic attack.

THE TRAIL OF TEARS

In the early days of America's history, both white settlers and Native Americans committed crimes, but the real victims were the tribes forced off their lands. One of the saddest events was the long journey taken by the Cherokees in 1838 from Georgia and North Carolina to the Indian Territory in Oklahoma. Some whites even jeered at them along the way. This became known as "The Trail of Tears" because of the Cherokees' suffering, including thousands of deaths, on the journey. A few Cherokees hid in the mountains of North Carolina and still have a reservation there.

crimes increased sevenfold in Britain in the first few months and included vandalism in a London synagogue. In Saskatoon, in the Canadian province of Saskatchewan, a Jewish library was set on fire. Several incidents occurred in Russia, including an attack by nearly 50 youths on a rabbi in Kiev while they chanted, "Kill the Jews." In the Russian towns of Perm and Ulyanovsk, swastikas and the slogan "Death to the Jews" were painted on synagogues. In Belgium, arson attacks were made on a Jewish-owned bookstore and butcher's shop, while synagogues in Brussels and Antwerp suffered **Molotov cocktail** attacks.

ANTI-SEMITIC ATTACKS IN THE UNITED STATES

In the United States, the Ku Klux Klan and other extremist groups publish anti-Semitic propaganda in books and on Web sites. Louis Farrakhan, leader of the black religious organization, The Nation of Islam, has labeled some American Jews as "not real Jews," calling them a "synagogue of Satan." In 2002, the European-American Unity and Rights Organization (EURO), led by former KKK member David Duke, offered a book titled

Jewish Supremacist Hate and Hypocrisy, and an article was published on its Web site entitled, "How Israeli Terrorism and American Treason Caused the Sept[ember] 11, 2001 Attacks."

Serious attacks occur each year in the United States. In 1999, during a

New Yorkers turn out to protest a Ku Klux Klan demonstration on October 23, 1999. A court had ruled, however, that Klansmen could march only without masks, and just 17 were brave enough to show their faces.

Muslims in the United States gathered in New York City in 1999 for a United American-Muslim Day Parade. Since the terrorist attacks of September 11, 2001, Muslims have increasingly been the victims of hate attacks.

two-month period in California, a gunman fired at random at Jewish children and staff in a Los Angeles community center, and three synagogues in the Sacramento area were set on fire. Anti-Semitic incidents declined in the United States in 2001, with 1,432 acts reported, a decrease from 1,606 incidents in 2000. The Anti-Defamation League (ADL), a Jewish organization established in 1913 to combat anti-Semitism, keeps track of such statistics. It recorded the same number of acts of harassment (877) in both years, but a large decrease in vandalism, dropping from 729 incidents to 555, the lowest figure reported in 20 years. Serious incidents did occur in 2001, however. A synagogue in Tacoma, Washington, was the target of arson days after graffiti appeared on its wall blaming Jews for the terrorist attacks of September 11, 2001. A more common type of crime happened in Greensburg, Pennsylvania, where vandals attacked a Jewish cemetery, painting swastikas on headstones and overturning them.

MUSLIMS, HINDUS, AND SIKHS

Long-standing conflicts in India exist between Muslims, Hindus, and Sikhs. Mahatma Gandhi of India led a peaceful **civil disobedience** campaign to end Britain's rule of his country, but was assassinated in 1948 by a Hindu fanatic who objected to his kindness toward Muslims. In 1984, the prime minister of India, Indira Gandhi, was assassinated by her bodyguards, who were Sikhs, because she had sent troops to storm their Golden Temple. Hindus reacted by massacring over 3,000 Sikhs in Delhi.

The mainly Muslim areas of India became independent as the country of Pakistan in 1947, but since then, the different religions have led to constant tensions between the two countries, especially over the divided region of Kashmir. Both tested nuclear weapons in 1999, and by 2002, some one million troops had been deployed, facing one another along the line dividing Kashmir.

In the United States, Muslim Americans became major hate targets after September 11, 2001, even though the U.S. government moved quickly to protect them. President George W. Bush went to the Islamic Center in Washington, D.C., within a week to declare that the real face of Islam is peace. "America counts millions of Muslims among our citizens," he said, "and Muslims make an incredibly valuable contribution to our country. And they need to be treated with respect." U.S. Assistant Attorney General Ralph Boyd, Jr., warned that, "Any threats of violence or discrimination against Arab or Muslim Americans or Americans of South Asian descents are not just wrong and un-American, but also are unlawful and will be treated as such."

IGNORANCE: THE BREEDING GROUND FOR CRIMES OF HATE

Arab-Americans and other Middle Eastern peoples have become major targets of hate crimes because most racist Americans cannot identify the country their families came from. Someone from Turkey may be targeted because the attacker believes he or she is Iranian. Hate crimes against Arabs increased when hostages were taken at the U.S. embassy in Iran in 1979. They also rose during the 1991 Gulf War against Iraq. A record number of attacks occurred after September 11, 2001, with the Council on American-Islamic Relations recording more than 700 possible hate crimes the first month following the terrorist attacks. On September 15, 2001, three killings occurred: an Egyptian was shot in his shop in San Gabriel, California; a Pakistani was shot in his grocery store; and a Sikh was shot outside his gas station by a man in a passing truck.

Incidents that are more serious have occurred. Windows were broken at an Islamic bookstore in Alexandria, Virginia, by bricks wrapped with messages vowing "death to Arab murderers." In Irving, Texas, six bullets were fired through windows of the Islamic Center, causing about $2,000 worth of damage. Other windows were broken at **mosques** in Carrollton, Texas, and San Francisco. A car was rammed into the front of an Arab-American grocery store in San Antonio, Texas, and the Nation of Islam mosque was set on fire in Austin, Texas. Muslims and their properties were

Muslim men pray at the Masjid Al-Farooq Mosque in Colorado Springs, Colorado, on November 2, 2001. Their religion has come under attack after extremist Muslims brought terrorism onto American soil.

also attacked in Europe, including Britain, where some mosques have been accused of promoting Islamic terrorism.

Religious hate crimes are found in other parts of the world, even against Christians in general. The Chinese government arrested 130 members (including three Americans) of the Fang-Cheng Christian

A Muslim girl takes part in a protest outside the Pakistani embassy in London on September 18, 2001. The scare headline shows the tensions after September 11, 2001.

THE BRANCH DAVIDIAN CULT

Religious cults are organizations with different religious practices from those of recognized church denominations. A cult is usually built around the personality of its leader. Americans are suspicious of cults, since some leaders have had an almost hypnotic power over their followers. Those in a cult often believe outsiders commit hate crimes against them. In 1978, all 913 members (including 240 children) of the People's Temple of the Disciples of Christ, a U.S. cult in Guyana, committed suicide when their leader, Jim Jones, ordered them to drink poison.

David Koresh, who claimed to be a prophet, led the Branch Davidians. Based in Waco, Texas, they collected guns and explosives because of their fear of the government and conventional society. When four federal agents tried to force their way into the building in 1993, they were shot and killed.

Federal officers then began a 51-day siege before ramming the building with armored vehicles and firing tear gas. The Branch Davidians started a fire in the building, which killed about 80 of the cult members, including Koresh. Eleven surviving members were found not guilty of murdering the agents. They continued to believe the government had committed a religious hate crime against them.

Evangelical Church in 2000. After the American-led air strikes on Afghanistan in 2002, a Christian church was attacked in Behawalpur, Pakistan. Five masked men opened fire, killing the minister and 15 others, including two Americans. The Protestant congregation had worshiped in the church for 30 years. Its parish priest said, "When something happens with America, they attack Christian churches."

Political and Social Hatred

Many types of hate crimes grow out of hatred for a nation, a political system, or a social class. This includes such acts as assassinations, terrorism, and attacks on people and institutions for economic, ethical, or other reasons.

Assassinations of political leaders can bring sorrow to nations and change the course of history. The assassination of President John F. Kennedy in 1963 in Dallas put the United States and much of the world into mourning, although news reports did show a few people celebrating Kennedy's death because they opposed his politics. The police soon arrested Lee Harvey Oswald, an American who had been a Communist and lived in Russia. Two days later, Jack Ruby shot and killed Oswald while he was in police custody. This murder of the young, idealistic president was one of America's greatest tragedies, but it changed the political scene in a positive way. The nation was so shocked and angry that Congress, under the urging of the new president, Lyndon B. Johnson, soon passed Kennedy's program of helping racial minorities and the poor.

Left: Wearing masks, members of the Basque Young Socialist Party chain themselves to the railings of the Basque parliament building in Vitoria, northern Spain. Their protest on June 28, 2002, was against the Basque terrorist group, ETA.

POLITICAL HATE CRIMES

Kennedy's younger brother, Robert, was another victim of a political hate crime. He was the U.S. Attorney General and had strongly enforced laws that protected civil rights. While campaigning for president in 1968, five years after his brother was assassinated, Robert Kennedy was shot and killed in Los Angeles by Sirhan Sirhan, a young Palestinian American who was furious that the United States supported Israel. This political motive surprised most Americans, who would not have linked Kennedy directly to the Israeli cause. Two months later, in June, Martin Luther King, Jr. was assassinated. This racial hate crime is discussed further in Chapter Five.

The country's first assassinated president was Abraham Lincoln, shot in Ford's Theater in Washington, D.C., by the actor John Wilkes Booth who sympathized with the South, which had just lost the Civil War. In this case, however, the nation's grief was turned against the former Confederate states, and Lincoln's planned program to be kind to the former enemy and bring them quickly back into the Union was replaced by a strict and long military occupation of the South.

Some U.S. politicians at the state level have been assassinated because of their outrageous conduct and shady political deals. Huey Long was the governor of Louisiana (1928–1932) and became so powerful that he ruled the state like a dictator. People called him the "Kingfish." Although he made economic and social reforms to help poor people, Long mostly helped himself. When he was senator, Franklin D. Roosevelt called him one of the most dangerous men in America, saying that Long could start a revolution. One month after Long announced he would run for president, he was assassinated in 1935 on his capitol's steps by a physician, Dr. Karl Weiss, the son of a man Long had treated badly.

POLITICAL ASSASSINATIONS—PAST AND PRESENT

Assassinations in other countries have also affected the United States and the world. In fact, World War I began because Archduke Franz Ferdinand

The Civil War was followed by one of the nation's worst hate crimes. The actor John Wilkes Booth, who supported the South, shot President Abraham Lincoln in Ford's Theater in Washington, D.C., on April 14, 1865; Lincoln died the next morning.

Assassinations have been the supreme crime of political hate. Austria's Archduke Franz Ferdinand and his wife were killed on June 28, 1914, by a Serbian in Sarajevo. This act began a series of events that led to World War I.

was shot and killed, along with his wife, in 1914 in Sarajevo, the capital of Bosnia-Herzegovina. Ferdinand was the heir to the throne of Austria-Hungary, which had annexed this area. His assassin was a Bosnian student. The attack was linked to a terrorist group in Serbia, which wanted the territory. Austria-Hungary declared war on Serbia, and other countries joined both sides, starting one of the largest wars in history. On April 6, 1917, the United States joined the Allies, who were victorious 19 months later, in November 1918.

Assassins have also killed foreign leaders who were peacemakers. Anwar Sadat of Egypt is the only Arab leader to sign a peace treaty with Israel, and he shared the 1978 Nobel Peace Prize with Prime Minister Menachem Begin of Israel. Much of this happened because President Jimmy Carter brought the two men together at Camp David that year. Muslim extremists disliked these peace movements, and they assassinated Sadat in 1981 while he was reviewing his troops.

Another tragic death was that of Prime Minister Yitzhak Rabin of Israel. He signed a historic agreement with the terrorist Palestinian Liberation Organization (PLO) in 1993, in which Israel recognized the PLO as the Palestinians' representative and the Palestinians recognized Israel's right to exist. Rabin then signed a peace treaty with Jordan in 1994 in Washington, D.C., ending a 46-year state of war. That year, he shared the Nobel Peace Prize with Yasser Arafat, the PLO leader, and Shimon Peres, Israel's former prime minister. Because of this, Rabin was shot and killed in 1995 while attending a peace rally in Tel Aviv. The attacker was a young Israeli extremist who opposed compromise with the Arabs.

ANARCHISTS: UNDERMINING ORGANIZED SOCIETY

Terrorists have also taken many lives. In the early 20th century, people usually thought of terrorists as **anarchists**—people who want to end organized society and its controlling government. Anarchists sometimes tossed bombs into crowds to disrupt an event. An assassin, like the one who

Israel's prime minister, Yitzhak Rabin, was assassinated by a Jewish fanatic on November 4, 1995, in Tel Aviv. Rabin had signed a peace treaty with the Palestinians, for which he became a victim within his own country.

THE UNABOMBER

The FBI's "Unabomber" case was an unusual hate crime that became the Bureau's longest and most expensive hunt for a serial bomber. An unknown man sent mail bombs to people from coast to coast for 18 years, killing three people and injuring 29. The FBI used the name "Unabomber" because the bombs were first sent to universities and airlines. Finally, the killer wrote to *The New York Times* and *The Washington Post,* promising to stop the bombs if they would print his 35,000-word manifesto explaining his reasons.

They did, and this led to the capture of Theodore Kaczynski when his brother, David, recognized his thoughts and expressions in the newspaper and called the FBI. Kaczynski was living like a hermit in a cabin in the Montana woods. He had a degree from

Harvard University and was considered a mathematical genius. However, he came to hate technology and sent bombs to those involved in it. His manifesto said the Industrial Revolution had been a disaster for the human race, because it made life unfulfilling and severely damaged the natural world. On January 22, 1998, Kaczynski changed his plea to guilty in exchange for a life sentence in prison without the possibility of parole.

started World War I, is not a terrorist who wants to kill civilians. Gradually, political movements and even nations adopted terrorist tactics against their enemies or to publicize their causes.

The first major international terrorist event involving Americans began on November 4, 1979, when Iranian students stormed the U.S. embassy in their country and took about 90 hostages, including 63 Americans. They wanted the United States to return Iran's former shah (ruler) for trial. He was having medical treatment in New York City after the strict Islamic religious leader, Ayatollah Khomeini, forced him out of Iran. The militant Iranians showed the hostages led around in blindfolds, and Americans at home were outraged. Some attacked Iranians living or studying in the United States. President Jimmy Carter approved a rescue plan by the military, but this failed, and eight Americans were killed and five wounded. After 444 days, the hostages were released when Ronald Reagan was inaugurated in 1981. The shah had died six months earlier in Egypt.

Kidnappings and hijackings of planes were common terrorist crimes in the 1980s. In Lebanon, Islamic extremists kidnapped citizens from the United States, Britain, France, and the U.S.S.R. All were released safely by 1992, some having been held for years. As many as 1,000 terrorist incidents were recorded in 1988, and more victims were murdered. In 1983, a truck bomb destroyed the U.S. embassy in Lebanon, killing 40, including 17 Americans. Then, five months later, a suicide bomber attacked the U.S. Marine headquarters in Beirut, Lebanon, killing 241 Americans. Another truck bomb that day killed 58 French paratroopers.

The world was shocked on December 21, 1988, when Pan American Airlines Flight 103 from London to New York exploded over Lockerbie, Scotland, because of a bomb. All 259 people on board the Boeing 747 were killed, as were 11 more on the ground. A long investigation included FBI and CIA agents and led to a Libyan intelligence officer. A Scottish court meeting in The Netherlands tried him and found him guilty on January 31, 2001. He was sentenced to life in prison in Scotland.

An engineer examines the remains of the Pan Am 747 jumbo jet bombed by Libyan terrorists on December 21, 1988, killing 270 people. Airliners were used for acts of terrorism long before the atrocities of September 11, 2001.

THE ATROCITIES OF SEPTEMBER 11, 2001, AND OKLAHOMA CITY

The worst terrorist atrocity in history occurred on September 11, 2001, when Islamic terrorists hijacked four Boeing jetliners. They flew two of them, with five hijackers in each plane, into New York's World Trade Center, killing more than 3,000 people when the towers collapsed. (By May 2002, officials had identified 2,823 of the victims.) Five more terrorists flew a jetliner into the Pentagon in Washington, D.C., causing 189 deaths and massive damage, and four others hijacked a flight that crashed near Shanksville, Pennsylvania, killing all 45 on board after the passengers fought back.

Although the terrorists were Muslim extremists, these crimes were done to injure the United States' political and economic leadership. The Afghanistan-based Al Qaeda terrorist organization, led by Osama bin Laden, committed the acts primarily in revenge for America's worldwide influence and the American government's support of Israel. Bin Laden left his native Saudi Arabia to fight against the Soviet forces in Afghanistan. He became a true terrorist after becoming upset that U.S. forces were in Saudi Arabia to defend his country in 1991 during the Gulf War against Iraq.

Hate crimes against the American government also come from within the country. The worst event happened on April 19, 1995, in Oklahoma City when Timothy McVeigh left a truck bomb in front of the federal building and 168 people, including 19 children, were killed by the explosion. McVeigh was quickly caught, tried, and executed, and a man who assisted him received life in prison. McVeigh, like members of many paramilitary or "survivalist" groups, believed the government was using its power to control its citizens.

Ground Zero reflects the evil and tragedy of human hatred. It also is a symbol of rebirth and the American spirit. By the first anniversary of September 11, 2001, New Yorkers were planning the site's future. It will include a memorial to those who died and a magnificent new building.

CHARLES MANSON

Charles Manson, leader of the hippie cult that turned to murder, was born in 1934 in Kentucky and committed an armed robbery when he was 13. He tried writing songs, but failed. In 1960, he was sent to prison for a series of crimes. Released in 1967, he began his commune of hippies at a ranch outside Los Angeles. He had a strong personality and power over his friends, but his thoughts were strange. He read special meanings into the Beatles' lyrics and decided to conduct a class war, drawing up the names of "pigs" to be murdered.

On August 9, 1979, Manson sent his group to Los Angeles to kill middle-class residents. They broke into the home of the pregnant actress Sharon Tate (the wife of the Polish film director Roman Polanski, who was in London) and killed her, three guests, and a passerby. Later, they killed another couple. Manson and five members of his cult were sentenced to death, but this was changed to life in prison. One of his female followers tried to assassinate President Gerald Ford in 1975, but was jailed. Manson has tried several times to be paroled, without success.

THE MANSON GANG AND THE STORY OF THE SLA

Another type of crime is based on the hate people have for certain members or classes of society. This was the reason for many violent acts in the 1960s. Charles Manson sent his cult "family" of hippies into a rich neighborhood of Los Angeles in 1969 to murder four people, one being the actress Sharon Tate. His group believed that their rejection of society justified their violence. Manson and five of his followers were sentenced to death, but California dropped the death penalty and the sentences became life in prison, where Manson remains to this day.

Charles Manson is an infamous example of a cult leader driven by social hatred. He caused the deaths of seven middle-class people. His crimes shocked many Americans, turning them against the hippie movement.

Caught on camera in 1974, Patricia Hearst, the kidnapped heiress, helps rob a bank with her SLA comrades. Some claim she was brainwashed. When finally captured by the police, she was put on trial for grand theft and was convicted.

Another organization fighting the class war in California was known as the Symbionese Liberation Army (SLA). In 1974, they kidnapped Patricia Hearst, called "Patty," the daughter of the rich newspaper owner Randolph Hearst, to force him to distribute $2 million of free food to the poor. After this was done, Patty strangely decided to join the terrorists and even helped them rob a bank. When the FBI and 400 police surrounded the gang's Los Angeles hideout, six members died in a fire caused by the shooting. Hearst, however, was not found and arrested until 16 months later, in 1975. She was sentenced to five years in prison, but served only 22 months because President Jimmy Carter **commuted** her sentence.

However, it is not just the rich or influential who are targeted. Hate crimes are also committed against poor members of society. Many homeless "street people" are attacked each year, and are harassed, kicked, set on fire, and even beaten to death. It is possible that such attacks are motivated not by hate, but simply because vulnerable street people make soft targets.

TEACHING TOLERANCE

Racial tensions were building at San Clemente High School in California in the 1990s. A white student was killed in 1993 during an off-campus fight between white and Latino students. Soon after, Joe Moros, a teacher at the school, designed and began teaching a class entitled, "Promoting Tolerance Through Understanding." It brought together students of all races to discuss prejudices, and this personal interaction produced amazing results.

"I have seen budding bigots change their outlooks in weeks," Moros said. The success has led him to teach the class in other high schools, and he believes the subject should be taught as part of every school's curriculum.

THE COLUMBINE HIGH SCHOOL SHOOTING

Sometimes, a hate crime is directed at certain cliques (exclusive circles) in society that someone else may feel is snobbish and trying to keep him or her out. This had tragic results at Columbine High School in Littleton, Colorado, when two students brought guns to school in 1999 and killed 12 fellow students and a teacher and wounded 30 more people before committing suicide. Their weapons were a rifle, two shotguns, and a handgun. They began shooting in the school's parking lot and moved through the cafeteria, hallways, and library.

The attackers were two seniors, Eric Harris, 17, and Dylan Klebold, 18. They were members of an outcast group who wore long black coats and called themselves "The Trenchcoat Mafia." Some students admitted that the rest of the school ostracized (would not associate with) members of the group. Harris and Klebold particularly hated the popular football players and other athletes. When they entered the school library with their guns, one yelled, "All jocks stand up! We're going to kill every one of you." A state commission later criticized school officials for not acting on the two students' antisocial behavior.

From 1999 through 2001, there were 109 recorded murders of homeless people in the United States (not by other street people, but by people who had homes). And 140 other violent crimes were reported in 82 cities during the same period.

THE ANTIGLOBALIZATION MOVEMENT

Class and economics have caused much larger hate crimes. An international example is the anticapitalist, **antiglobalization** movement. The antiglobalization movement protests against big-business exploitation of labor in developing countries, and the harmful effects that this has on both the environment and communities. In 1998, some 40,000 protesters arrived in Geneva, Switzerland, to protest the World Trade Organization's (WTO) meeting there. They threw bottles and paint bombs at banks and other corporation buildings, causing $3 million in damages.

Two years later, tens of thousands of these protesters gathered in Seattle from around the world and delayed the beginning of the WTO meeting, breaking windows of nearly every downtown store and covering buildings in graffiti. Seattle's 1,800-strong police force had to use tear gas, pepper spray, rubber bullets, and curfews to end the riots.

Other attacks are committed, the offenders say, for ethical reasons. Abortion clinics and their doctors and nurses have been attacked by "right to life" demonstrators who are usually linked to a religious group. The National Abortion Federation recorded five murders and 1,700 acts of violence between 1977 and 1994. Clinics were still bombed throughout the 1990s, including ones in Atlanta and Tulsa in 1997 and in Birmingham, Alabama, in 1998. An abortion doctor, Barnett Slepian, of Amherst, New York, was harassed with signs in front of his home saying "Slepian Kills Children," and on October 23, 1998, he was killed by a sniper's bullet while in his home.

Another "ethical area" is animal rights. Crimes by activists have ranged from arson attacks on laboratories and universities that conduct animal

Animal rights activists stage protests in Seoul, Korea, on May 30, 2002, before the soccer World Cup Finals began. People for the Ethical Treatment of Animals (PETA) was opposing the killing of dogs in Korea for human consumption.

research experiments to placing bombs in the cars of scientists and professors. In 2001, in Spain, Germany, and The Netherlands, animal rights activists released more than 40,000 mink. That same year, an animal rights activist was sentenced to a mental hospital in Britain for sending 15 letter bombs to businesses and people working with animals, injuring two adults and one child.

About 60,000 antiglobalization activists gather in Genoa, Italy, on July 20, 2002, on the first anniversary of a demonstrator's death. He had been shot by police while protesting an economic summit there the previous year.

Sexual Hatred

Crimes that involve hatred of a sexual nature are normally committed against homosexuals and women. The Hate Crimes Prevention Act debated in 2002 in Congress would make violence because of sexual orientation or gender a federal crime.

Twenty-four states and the District of Columbia have hate crime laws that include sexual orientation. Crimes against gays, formally called homophobic crimes, seem to be increasing. About 16 percent of the incidents recorded in the FBI's Hate Crime Statistics for 2000 involved sexual orientation. This is lower than the true figure, however, because victims seldom report such a crime, since many people do not want to reveal they are homosexual.

One study found that 41 percent of gay adults had been a victim of a hate crime of one kind or another. A survey in Massachusetts found that 72 percent of lesbian girls had been called offensive names. Physical attacks on gays are usually more violent than those against other minorities. In 2002, in Montana, a lesbian couple and their child luckily escaped after someone set their house on fire.

GAY RIGHTS

A tragic example was the killing in 1999 of Matthew Shepard, an openly gay young man in Wyoming who was beaten by two men and left to die. (Anonymous hate messages by e-mail to gay organizations in Fort Collins, Colorado, soon followed, with one saying, "I hope it happens more often.")

Left: Sexual hatred often centers on gays. These two gay rights activists are among some 10,000 people participating in an annual parade in Mexico City to demand an end to sexual discrimination and call for equal rights for gays and lesbians.

Hate can survive death. A demonstrator protests against homophobia in Casper, Wyoming, during the funeral of Matthew Shepard, a University of Wyoming student kidnapped and murdered because he was gay.

Wyoming had no hate crimes law. Former president Bill Clinton said, "I was deeply grieved by the act of violence perpetrated against Matthew Shepard. There is nothing more important to the future of this country than our standing together against intolerance, prejudice, and violent bigotry." Former president Clinton was a strong supporter of gay rights. In 1995, he introduced a "Don't Ask, Don't Tell" policy to allow gays and lesbians to remain in the armed forces (although harassment still exists).

Gay rights activists taking part in a parade in Reforma Avenue in Mexico City, June 29, 2002. Some 10,000 people took part in the annual parade against discrimination and to demand equal rights for gays and lesbians. Gay parades celebrating gay culture also occur in many other major cities, including Berlin, Germany, and Sydney, Australia.

MATTHEW SHEPARD

Matthew Shepard was a gay student at the University of Wyoming. He had traveled in several countries and spoke German and Italian. In 1998, two men posing as homosexuals met Shepard in a bar, lured him outside, and kidnapped him, driving him into the countryside. There, they beat him with a pistol and left him tied to a fence in the cold night. He died five days later in a hospital.

The two men were soon caught. Russell Henderson and Aaron McKinney, both 21, pleaded guilty and were sentenced to life in prison without parole. During the trial, Henderson said, "There is not a moment that goes by that I don't see what happened that night," and told Shepard's parents and his own mother and father, "I hope one day you will be able to find it in your heart to forgive me."

The terrible crime inspired demands in several states for hate crime laws protecting homosexuals. Shepard's parents went to

Washington, D.C., to plead with Congress to pass the Hate Crime Prevention Act with protection for homosexuals. Former president Bill Clinton urged Congress to pass the act. "By doing so," he said, "this will help make all Americans more safe and secure."

Homophobia of such an aggressive and unpleasant nature is difficult to eradicate. Education and the nuturing of a tolerant, open society are the way forward—but this will always mean that extremists will be able to have their say.

Sexual harassment in the office is often a hate crime done to make the victim feel helpless and insignificant. This is a serious problem that is being tackled by educational programs and recent court rulings.

Three years later, he signed an executive order that banned discrimination against gays and lesbians in the federal workplace.

Sometimes, antihomosexual statements and laws encourage hate crimes against gays. This is especially true during campaigns against gays, such as the religious one launched in 1976 by the popular celebrity Anita Bryant, and the 1983 warnings about homosexuals and AIDS given by Jerry Falwell, religious leader of the Moral Majority movement.

Several states still have laws that discriminate against gays, such as Florida's ban on lesbians and gays adopting a child. This became law in 1977 during the crusade by Bryant, who lived in Florida. A federal judge in Miami upheld the law in 2001.

Other campaigns seek to change people from homosexuals to heterosexuals. A series of full-page ads in 1998 in major national newspapers, like *The New York Times* and *USA Today,* were headlined "Toward Hope and Healing for Homosexuals." The ads, run by

WOMEN AT THE CITADEL

The Citadel in South Carolina, a top military school, was shocked in 1993 when a woman, Shannon Faulkner, applied to join its cadet corps. The school fought a three-year court battle to maintain its all-male tradition, but lost a Supreme Court decision. Faulkner received death threats in addition to other forms of harassment.

On campus at last, she was called rude names and harassed in other ways. After five days, she dropped out, ill and upset. Faulkner had opened the legal door, however, and in 1996, the Citadel dropped its 153-year-old ban on women. The first woman graduated in 1999 and many others have followed her example since then.

Although women are an integral part of the United States armed forces, The Citadel military college in Charleston, South Carolina, opposed women cadets until it lost a Supreme Court ruling. Here, a female officer in the Arizona National Guard gives orders to a subordinate.

conservative religious groups, said there is a "way out" for gays.

Some organizations discriminate against homosexuals to protect their members. The best-known example is the Boy Scouts, who ban leaders and members from being openly homosexual. This was upheld in 2000 by the U.S. Supreme Court, which said a private organization has the right to restrict its membership. Other groups disagreed with the Scouts, including local United Way charities, which protested by withholding their donations to the Scouts.

Hate crimes against homosexuals are a worldwide problem, occurring from London, England, where a pub frequented by gays was bombed, to Zimbabwe, whose outspoken president, Robert Mugabe, has called homosexuals "worse than dogs and pigs."

THE STRUGGLE CONTINUES

The other well-known sexual hate crime is the intimidation, harassment, and violence against women. The 1994 Violence Against Women Act provided for the education and training of law enforcement officials and prosecutors to handle these crimes, and it approved crisis centers for domestic violence. The law also established the right of victims of gender-based violent crimes to receive compensation. In 1972, Congress passed an Equal Rights Amendment to the Constitution to make women equal under law, but it needed 38 states to approve it by 1982. The amendment failed when only 35 states gave approval.

Some types of sexual harassment of women are true hate crimes when done to insult or belittle the victim. Most women do not report harassment in the workplace because any complaints might harm their careers. A 1995 report by the Pentagon said that 78 percent of all women in the military have been sexually harassed. Another survey by the National Organization for Women (NOW) found that 89 percent of girls and women had been sexually harassed in school. The U.S. government forced the Citadel military school in South Carolina to admit women cadets in 1996, but the first one accepted resigned after suffering harassment.

NOW, founded in 1966 by **feminist** Betty Friedan, campaigns constantly against the sexual oppression of women, including all forms of violence. It also runs campaigns against racism and homophobia, the fear or hatred of homosexuals.

STALKING, OBSESSION, AND MURDER

A more dangerous crime is stalking, which is following a person around. Anyone can be a target, but the few cases that have received nationwide attention involved celebrities, including the singer Madonna and movie star Jodie Foster. Indeed, the man obsessed by Foster tried to gain her attention by making an attempt on the life of the president, Ronald Reagan. In Britain, the popular television personality Jill Dando was shot and killed on her doorstep in 1999 by a man who lived nearby. The killer, the evidence showed, was obsessed with Dando, often called "television's golden girl," and had previously stalked her.

Serial killer Theodore Bundy began by stalking women, but did not attack them. Many serial killers of women have developed a hatred for that sex because of experiences in their lives. Bundy, who supposedly killed 23 victims, was born illegitimate. His mother, who showed little affection for him, first told Bundy that he was her brother to cover up her shame. When he found out his true relationship, he was shocked. Some serial killers believe all women are evil, which seemed to be the motive of Jack the Ripper in London in 1888.

This type of random murder of strangers is difficult to solve. In Vancouver, Canada, 50 women have disappeared during the 20 years from 1982 to 2002 without the killer being caught. In Seattle, 120 miles away, the bodies of 49 women were discovered from 1982 to 1989, and a man was arrested only in 2002. Also in 2002, women's groups in Mexico and the United States called for a task force to investigate the murders of hundreds of women in Ciudad Juarez, a Mexican border town.

The writer and feminist Betty Friedan founded the National Organization for Women (NOW) that campaigns to reduce violence against women and minorities. She travels throughout the country to promote this message.

Demonstrators celebrated when serial killer Ted Bundy was executed in Florida's electric chair on January 24, 1989. He confessed to murdering 23 women and was regarded by other prisoners as the lowest type of criminal.

THEODORE BUNDY

America's infamous serial killer, Theodore Bundy, was born in 1946 in Vermont. His first emotional blow was finding out that his mother was unmarried when he was born. He never knew who his father was and had to live with his violent grandfather. Still, Bundy became known for his charm, and several people thought he would make a good politician. He worked as a salesman in a department store and began stealing. He loved a rich society girl, but she turned him down, and most of his victims were college girls in Washington, Oregon, Utah, and Colorado who resembled her.

Bundy, who was known as Ted, was handsome and intelligent, studying psychology and law at Stanford University. His first murder was in 1974, and several more followed before he was caught and tried in 1977. However, he escaped and went to Florida. He took a new name of Christopher Hagen, and in 1978, murdered a 12-year-old schoolgirl in Pensacola. Police found his abandoned stolen van full of evidence and soon arrested him. His trial in 1979 was televised, and Bundy acted as his own lawyer. He was found guilty and sentenced to death. In 1989, after several appeals, he was executed in the electric chair.

Race Hatred

In the United States, when we hear about crimes of prejudice, we probably think of the struggles of African Americans and other racial minorities. America is truly the land of many races, with most living in peace and friendship. However, racial hatred and associated crimes have never gone away.

Crimes have been committed against African Americans since the first slaves arrived in the colonies in 1619. It took nearly 250 years for that evil institution to be abolished finally by the Civil War and Lincoln's Emancipation Proclamation. Even then, the former slaves faced hate crimes from whites who considered black people ignorant and lazy. The worst attacks came from the Ku Klux Klan, established in 1866 to uphold white supremacy in the South. It was not until civil rights laws were passed after World War II that African Americans had an opportunity to participate more fully in the American dream.

AMERICA'S HISTORY OF RACIAL HATRED

Other minorities were also treated badly. The British, Spanish, and French settlers moved the **indigenous** peoples of America on to reservations. Pioneers took away their lands and killed their buffalo, backed by soldiers following rumors or newspaper reports of Indians massacring whites. The Indian Wars reduced a proud people to virtual prisoners on reservations. The Chinese were also considered worthless by whites until the Central Pacific Railroad line hired 11,000 to build the first transcontinental

Left: The peaceful civil rights movement was in contrast to the racial violence experienced in many U.S. cities. During the 1960s, buildings were burned and looted in Los Angeles, Detroit, and Newark, New Jersey.

railroad line. Most people thought this was a joke, because the "coolies" spoke a different language, had another religion, and were too small. The Chinese proved them wrong, however, and won respect for "John Chinaman."

Some race crimes perpetrated by the government continued into the mid-19th century. An obvious example is the system of segregation that kept blacks and whites separated by law in the South and by tradition in the North. A decision by the U.S. Supreme Court ended this in 1954. The government also forced at least 110,000 Japanese Americans to live in detention camps similar to prison camps during World War II, fearing they

Martin Luther King, Jr. (second row by window) enjoyed bus rides after his boycott in Montgomery, Alabama, ended segregation on local buses. The practice was first challenged when Rosa Parks refused to sit in the back of a bus.

A police dog attacks a demonstrator for civil rights in Birmingham, Alabama, on May 3, 1963. Police also used high-pressure water hoses and arrested Martin Luther King, Jr., who wrote his famous "Letter from a Birmingham Jail."

"MISSISSIPPI BURNING"

The FBI's first case of investigating a racial crime was in 1964, after their participation was allowed by the Civil Rights Act of that year. The case involved the murder of three civil rights workers in June that year near Philadelphia, Mississippi: one African American, James Chaney, and two Jews, Michael Schwerner and Andrew Goodman. They had disappeared while investigating the burning of a black church, and their bodies were found buried in an earthen dam.

The agency named the case "Mississippi Burning," which was shortened to MIBURN, and it became the largest federal investigation ever conducted in that state. It proved difficult because the guilty people resisted the agents and blacks were too frightened to talk. The FBI's hard work, however, led to the

conviction of seven white racists on October 20, 1967, for "conspiring to violate the constitutional rights" of the slain men. The seven were given prison sentences ranging from 3 to 10 years. In 1988, a movie was made about the case, entitled *Mississippi Burning.* Gene Hackman and Willem Dafoe played the two agents.

would somehow help Japan during the conflict. Many Japanese Americans, however, proved their patriotism by serving in the U.S. armed forces as translators who could interview prisoners and listen to the enemy's radio messages.

Crimes against minorities since the 1950s have been committed by individuals or hate groups. Blacks suffered the most in the 1960s during the civil rights movement led by Martin Luther King, Jr. and other black leaders. The Ku Klux Klan and other white supremacist organizations, such as the White Citizens' Council, opposed them. In 1968, James Earl Ray, a white man, assassinated King, and other African Americans were murdered, including an official of the National Association for the Advancement of Colored People (NAACP). Some blacks reacted by rioting in several cities and supporting extremist black groups, such as the Black Panthers and the Black Muslims, whose spokesman was Malcolm X.

THE PROBLEM HAS NEVER GONE AWAY

Even today, dreadful racial crimes occur each year. Americans were shocked in 1998 when three white men killed James Byrd, a black man, by dragging him behind their pickup truck near Jasper, Texas. All three were convicted, with two given death sentences and the other sentenced to life in prison. A widespread series of arson attacks on black churches in the South also happened in the 1990s, and President Bill Clinton set up a special group known as the National Church Arson Task Force (NCARF). It was made up of agents from the FBI and the Bureau of Alcohol, Tobacco, and Firearms, as well as lawyers from the U.S. Department of Justice's Civil Rights Division. In June 1997, the task force reported that its work had led to convictions of 110 people in connection with 77 church fires.

The FBI's Hate Crime Statistics for 2000 shows that race crimes make up 54 percent of the incidents, by far the largest portion. This does not include crimes against a person's ethnic or national origin, which are 12 percent. Sometimes, it is difficult to decide which category a crime falls

Malcolm X addressed Black Muslims on December 1, 1963, saying that President John Kennedy's assassination was an example of "the chickens coming home to roost." Malcolm X, who preached violence, was assassinated by another African Americans in 1965.

Each time the Ku Klux Klan announces plans to march in cities, people mount a demonstration, like this group in New York City. The Klan uses the American right of freedom of speech to express its messages of hate.

under. Would Jewish people be religious, racial, or ethnic victims? The answer seems to be that it depends on the reason for the attack. The first person convicted under New York State's new Hate Crimes Act was a man in Brooklyn. He approached a man of Pakistani descent on a subway platform on October 11, 2001 (three days after the law took effect), and yelled at him for not speaking Spanish, then called him an ethnic name and wounded him with a knife.

Besides the FBI and other federal agencies, many U.S. organizations fight racial crimes. The Southern Poverty Law Center in Montgomery, Alabama, records the nationwide incidents and keeps up with racist hate groups, compiling the "Klan Watch." The Center for Democratic Renewal in Atlanta established a system to link hundreds of local groups who are combating discrimination.

RACIAL HATE CRIMES ELSEWHERE

Other nations have shown an increase in race crimes. In 2002, a survey conducted for the British Broadcasting Corporation (BBC) found that 51 percent of Britons believe they live in a racist society. At the same time, 47 percent said immigration in the past half-century had harmed British society. The Institute of Race Relations in London said in 2002 that 25 race-motivated murders had happened since 1991 in the country. The Human Rights Watch noted that Britain has the highest incidents of racial crimes in Europe, with 120,000 estimated annually.

One highly publicized case involved the murder of Stephen Lawrence, a black teenager, who was stabbed in 1993 at a London bus stop by a gang of white youths. Although no one was ever charged with the crime, an independent investigation begun by the government issued a report in 1999 that criticized the London police force and others for having "institutional racism" in its ranks.

European racists have been encouraged by recent increases in votes for candidates that criticize the number of immigrants in their nations.

Burned-out cars in a street in Burnley in June 2001, following rioting by Asian youths, who were also involved in running battles with white youths. Some of the worst rioting the U.K. has seen in 20 years erupted in the summer months of 2001 in Oldham, Burnley, and Bradford in the north of England. "Shockingly" divided communities, goaded by far-right extremists, led to the summer riots, according to a government-commissioned report.

Vocal protesters gather in London on June 29, 1998, outside the building where the Stephen Lawrence inquiry was held. The inquiry was suspended because members of the black Nation of Islam disrupted the hearing.

However, this may have happened for other reasons. Jean-Marie Le Pen of France's National Front party won the second largest amount of votes in the first voting round of the 2002 national elections, but many voters were

THE NATION OF ISLAM

The Black Muslim movement was founded as the Nation of Islam in 1930 in Detroit and was led from 1934 to 1975 by African American Elijah Muhammad, who called himself "the messenger of Allah." The movement wanted to form another nation for blacks within the United States. One of the organization's greatest speakers was Malcolm X, who decided to leave and form his own group. He was shot and killed in 1965, and many believe the Black Muslims assassinated him. Muhammad's son, Wallace, became leader of the Nation of Islam in 1975 and turned it into a more traditional Muslim organization. Its name was changed to the World Community of Islam in the West and then to the American Muslim Mission.

Louis Farrakhan became the leader of a splinter group growing out of Muhammad's group in 1977, and it took the original name of the Nation of Islam. Farrakhan organized a "Million Man March" to Washington, D.C., to encourage blacks to give better support to their families and communities. In 1996, the U.S. government barred him from accepting Libyan aid. He has been outspoken in his prejudices against whites and Jews, and the British government in 2002 refused to let him enter the country.

bored with and cynical about current politics and stayed home. However, in the second round of voting, large numbers of voters turned out, appalled by the success of the National Front party, and gave the party opposed to the National Front a landslide victory.

Jean-Marie Le Pen, the right-wing National Front party French presidential candidate, holds up ballot papers during a press conference at the party's headquarters near Paris on May 3, 2002. Le Pen was soundly beaten in the second round of voting two days later.

Ethnic violence in Rwanda in 1994 resulted in more than 450,000 Tutsis and Hutus massacred by Hutu extremists. These Rwandan refugees emerge on April 19, 1997, from jungle hideouts in neighboring Zaire.

GLOSSARY

Anarchist: a person who wants to do away with organized society and government

Antiglobalization: against large companies or economies spreading into other nations

Assassination: the murder of a political leader

Asylum seekers: people, such as refugees, who ask to enter a foreign nation and receive protection

Bias: another name for prejudice

Bigotry: another word for prejudice

Civil disobedience: refusing, in a peaceful way, to obey a government policy or law

Commune: a group of people, like hippies, who all live and work together

Commute (v.): to change a penalty to another one that is less severe

Deport: to send someone out of a country by legal means

Feminist: anyone who actively supports women's causes

Gender: the sex of a person (male or female)

Harassment: to annoy persistently

Indigenous: occurring naturally in or native to a particular region or environment

Intimidation: making someone timid or fearful through the use of threats

Manifesto: a written statement declaring publicly the intentions, motives, or views of its issuer

Molotov cocktail: an explosive weapon; each "cocktail" is a bottle filled with gasoline and wrapped in a rag or plugged with a wick, then ignited and thrown

Mosque: Muslim house of worship

Propaganda: the spreading of ideas, information, or rumor for the purpose of helping or injuring an institution, a cause, or a person

Racism: a belief that race is the primary determinant of human traits and capacities and that racial differences produce an inherent superiority of a particular race

Segregated: separated, especially the system of keeping different races apart

Stereotype: oversimplified image that is always used for a type of people, whether true or not

Synagogue: Jewish house of worship

Xenophobia: fear of foreigners or foreign things

Zero tolerance: a law enforcement policy of cautioning or arresting people who commit small offenses, since these acts might encourage worse crimes

CHRONOLOGY

These are some of the worst riots in American history:

1849:　May 10, more than 10,000 people riot in New York City to protest the British actor William Charles' competition with the American actor Edwin Forrest; many are in Irish gangs, chanting "Down with the English hog"; 20 people die when militia opens fire.

1861:　April 19, gangs of Confederate sympathizers in Baltimore attack Union troops passing through the city and burn bridges to slow their progress; soldiers open fire and kill 12 people; four in the army die.

1863:　July 13, up to 50,000 people riot in New York City to protest the draft for the Civil War; whites kill about 105 blacks, whom they blame for the war; they also burn the draft office, a black church, and a black orphanage; Army troops join police to fight running battles through the city.

1863:　In Richmond, Virginia, women desperate to feed their families chant, "Bread! Bread! Bread!" and break store windows to loot food; they disperse after Confederate President Jefferson Davis climbs onto a wagon and says the mob's leaders will be shot within five minutes.

1886:　May 4, a labor meeting attacks up to 1,400 people in Chicago's Haymarket Square; when 180 police appear, someone throws a bomb, killing seven officers and four workers, while wounding 50 others; the police fire into the running crowd and arrest eight anarchists; four are later hanged.

1922:　June 22 and 23, a coal-mine strike in Herrin, Illinois, turns into violence that leads to 36 deaths.

1943:　June 21, a race riot begins in Detroit when whites protest the employment of blacks; this leaves 34 dead and about 700 injured.

1943:　Six people die in a riot in New York's Harlem district.

1962:   October 1, two people die and many are injured when 3,000 troops have to put down riots in Oxford, Mississippi, as James Meredith becomes the University of Mississippi's first black student.

1965:   August 11, black people living in Los Angeles' Watts district begin rioting after police arrest a black driver; about 12,000 National Guardsmen are called in as up to 10,000 people riot for six days, causing 34 deaths and $200 million in damages; about 4,000 people are arrested.

1967:   July 12–17, a riot by blacks kills 26 people and injures 1,500 in Newark, New Jersey.

1967:   July 20–23, a black riot in Detroit kills 40 and injures about 2,000, with fires leaving about 50,000 people homeless.

1968:   April 4, Martin Luther King, Jr.'s assassination leads to riots by blacks in 130 U.S. cities with at least 45 killed, about 20,000 people arrested, and $45 million in property damage.

1968:   August 26, outside the Democratic National Convention, anti-Vietnam war protesters clash with 20,000 Chicago police, National Guardsmen, and soldiers; 700 demonstrators are injured and 650 are arrested.

1992:   April 29, a riot begins in the black and Hispanic sections of Los Angeles in reaction to the acquittal of policemen who had been filmed beating a black motorist, Rodney King; the four-day riot kills 55, injures 2,300, and causes $1 billion in damages.

1999:   December 1 and 2, thousands of protestors against capitalism and globalization riot in Seattle, smashing windows downtown and throwing missiles at 1,800 police; 400 are arrested.

2001:   April 7, violent black protests in Cincinnati occur after a policeman shoots and kills an unarmed black youth; police make more than 100 arrests and a curfew is imposed from April 12–16.

FURTHER INFORMATION

Useful Web Sites

Anti-Defamation League's Hate Crime Prevention Act: www.adl.org/legislative_action/hatecrimes_briefing.html

The Center for Democratic Renewal: www.thecdr.org/cgi-bin/main/site.pl

FBI site for young people: www.fbi.kids/6th12th/6th12th.htm

The FBI's hate crimes page: jackson.fbi.gov/hq/cid/civilrights/hate.htm

National Coalition for the Homeless hate crimes page: www.nationalhomeless.org/cr00hatecrimes.html

National Organization for Women: www.now.org

Southern Poverty Law Center: www.splcenter.org

The U.S. Department of Justice's site for young people: www.usdoj.gov/crt/crim/overview.htm

Further Reading

Carnes, Jim. *Us and Them: A History of Intolerance in America.* New York: Oxford University Press, 1999.

D'Angelo, Laura. *Hate Crimes.* Broomall, Pennsylvania: Chelsea House Publishers, 2002.

Espero, Roman. *What Is a Hate Crime?* San Diego: Greenhaven Press, 2001.

Freemon, David K. *The Jim Crow Laws and Racism in American History.* Springfield, New Jersey: Enslow Publishers, 2000.

Landau, Elaine. *Osama bin Laden: A War Against the West.* New York: Twenty First Century Books, 2002.

Louis, Nancy. *United We Stand: The War on Terrorism.* Minneapolis: Abdo & Daughters, 2002.

Webster-Doyle, Terence. *Why is Everybody Always Picking on Us?: Understanding the Roots of Prejudice.* New York: Weatherhill, Inc., 2000.

Wheeler, Jill C. *September 11, 2001: The Day that Changed America.* Minneapolis: Abdo & Daughters, 2002.

About the Author

Dr. John D. Wright is an American writer and editor living in England. He has been a reporter for *Time* and *People* magazines in their London bureaus, covering such subjects as politics, crime, and social welfare. He has also been a journalist for the U.S. Navy and for newspapers in Alabama and Tennessee. He holds a Ph.D. degree in Communications from the University of Texas, taught journalism at three Southern universities, and was chairman of the Department of Mass Communications at Emory & Henry College in Virginia. In 2001, he published a dictionary, *The Language of the Civil War*, and an encyclopedia of space exploration is scheduled for publication in Great Britain. He has contributed to many reference books, including the Oxford University Press *New Dictionary of National Biography* (under production), Reader's Digest *Facts at Your Fingertips* (2001), and the *Oxford Guide to British and American Culture* (1999).

INDEX